Four Conversations

Aligning People and Purpose

A Concise Leadership Guide

Rod Brace

Four Conversations: Aligning People and Purpose
by Rod Brace

Printed in the United States of America

ISBN: 978-0-9789265-2-6

Edited by Leigh McLeroy/Words that Work

Published by Lucid Books a Transform Media Group company.

For more articles and books from Rod Brace visit:
www.rodbrace.com

First Things First

A few comments are appropriate before you dive in to *Four Conversations*. First, let me say a word about the subtitle of the book – *A Concise Leadership Guide*. I find that most books make a few key points about their subject and fill the remaining pages with examples, stories or academic justification. I left those examples, stories and extras out, focusing only on the key points. With the increasing popularity of abstract services that boil books down to a few pages, it appears busy leaders are looking for concise information.

The danger in writing a concise book, however, is that readers may pass too lightly over key concepts. As additional support, examples of the four conversations are provided in the appendix. You might find it helpful to first read the conversation examples in the appendix to get a sense of your conversation "destination."

The *Four Conversations* approach itself is contrary to many other popular leadership books. This book does not establish the leader as the focus of organizational solutions.

Instead, you'll find that *Four Conversations* is a focus on those we lead. You will be challenged to listen intently to your team. One-on-one conversations will become the primary tool of your trade. You may be faced with a paradigm that is entirely new to you regarding leadership: You will be challenged to become a "self-aware" leader.

A paradigm of greater employee trust is also offered. Many companies have relegated the employee to an interchangeable part of a bigger engine. If the "part" (person) doesn't fit the "machinery" (company), the part is replaced. In *Four Conversations* each individual is recognized as important and unique in their own way. They are trusted to know their strengths. Too often, leaders have attempted to precisely script employee behavior, vocabulary and movement. Rather than pointing individuals toward the desired outcome and letting their strengths play out, our scripting and control make them interchangeable cogs lacking in passion for the company and its purpose.

Perhaps an analogy will be helpful in describing this distinction. The geographic center of the contiguous United States is in the middle of a farmer's field about a mile outside of Lebanon, Kansas. Imagine that an email went out to the top 100 most successful leaders in the U.S. asking them to arrive at that point in the field on a specific day at a given time. If the email gave no further directions, each leader would use whatever means available to him or her, whether by car, plane, or four-wheeler, to arrive at the destination. Creativity and the application of their available talents and resources would be left to their discretion, making it an efficient process. On the other hand, if the email indicated all participants must approach from the East on I-70 and then use U.S. Route 281, the leaders would have fewer options. The process would be inefficient. *It is impossible to precisely control the passionate pursuit of a clearly understood purpose in the hands of a talented person. Excessive control dampens passion.*

In short, you are holding a different style of book with a different message, designed for leaders who are more interested in those they lead than themselves. If your desire is to build up the human spirit and align people of passion with organizational purpose – the conversation starts here.

"

"Let us make a special effort to stop communicating with each other, so we can have some conversation." – Judith Martin as Miss Manners

The Art of Conversation

I made the mistake once, and only once, of admitting to friends that I am a big fan of Jane Austen books. Only one man in the group admitted that he knew of the works of Ms. Austen and that was because his mother loved her books as well. He interpreted my confession to the other guys by explaining that Austen wrote books for "lonely old spinsters." Laughs quickly ensued, and while my first inclination was to fight back, as we all know, lovers of Jane Austen are far too civil to do so.

My attraction to Austen's great works such as *Emma* and *Pride and Prejudice* rests in the dialogue. I am intrigued by the notion that people could sit in endless hours of conversation regarding matters as trivial as the common cold:

"You seem to have forgotten Mrs. and Miss Bates," said Emma, "I have not heard one enquiry after them."

"Oh! The good Bateses – I am quite ashamed of myself; but you mention them in most of your letters. I hope they are quite well. Good old Mrs. Bates – I will call upon her to-morrow, and take my children. They are always so pleased to see my children. And that excellent Miss Bates! – such thorough worthy people! How are they, sir?"

"Why, pretty well, my dear, upon the whole. But poor Mrs. Bates had a bad cold about a month ago."

"How sorry I am! but colds were never so prevalent as they have been this autumn. Mr. Wingfield told me that he had never known them more general or heavy, except when it has been quite an influenza."

"That has been a good deal the case, my dear, but not to the degree you mention. Perry says that colds have been very general, but not so heavy as he has very often known them in November. Perry does not call it altogether a sickly season."

"No, I do not know that Mr. Wingfield considers it *very* sickly except –"

"Ah! my poor dear child, the truth is, that in London it is always a sickly season. Nobody is healthy in London, nobody can be. It is a dreadful thing to have you forced to live there; – so far off! – and the air so bad!" [From *Emma* by Jane Austen[1]]

[1] Jane Austen, Emma (New York: Barnes & Noble Books, Barnes & Noble Classics, 2004), pp. 96-97.

Conversation as an art form intrigues me. There was a time when conversation was interesting, entertaining and necessary to the connection of people and their world. It was indeed an art. Today, however, we are losing the art of conversation. Neither the cryptic sound bites of text messaging or disconnected "Hi how are you?" exchanges with neighbors demonstrate artistry or connectivity.

As a result, we know less about those around us. We may even draw shallow conclusions about the people in our office or community. Our beliefs go unexpressed and therefore unchallenged. We live in an isolated world of distant acquaintances and we are, in the end, less aligned as human beings.

Alignment is the foundation of meaningful accomplishment. When our actions are aligned with our beliefs, we become passionate forces for change. When a team is aligned around a shared goal, they become an efficient display of human potential. Alignment meshes with goals, creating impact. In the absence of alignment, people and the organizations they comprise wander aimlessly. Everything begins with meaningful conversation.

"

"Talking with you is sort of the conversational equivalent of an out of body experience." – Calvin and Hobbes by Bill Watterson, cartoonist

Aligning Conversation

The connection between alignment and conversation is often dismissed by leaders who fail to see the value in discussing goals with those directly involved in their accomplishment. Meaningful, aligning conversation takes time. When a team member lacks understanding a leader must slow down and converse in a way that links their actions with organizational purpose. Aligned people fulfill purpose. Conversation connects people and purpose.

By design, conversation is strategic – and strategic conversation is most effective one-on-one. Information can be shared with a large group of people, but that is not a conversation. In large groups, individuals assume self-imposed roles. Think about how difficult it is to share in front of a crowd a personal belief or a lack of understanding. In a group we tend to use dialogue designed to impress the group rather than connect with others. We interrupt to get our point across quickly for fear that someone else will make that point. We assume various group roles. In some settings we are outspoken, in others we are reserved. The dynamic of the large group often works to limit meaningful conversation, and as a result, the group is not optimally aligned.

In one-on-one conversation we are better able to reach deep levels of transparency and instill trust. Hearing directly from others we are more inclined to change our view. We are more trusting when we are allowed to invest in the conversation. We are more transparent in our thinking when speaking face-to-face. Conversation at this level brings with it a strong alignment of ideas. Do not underestimate the power of intimate conversation toward genuine alignment.

"

"Saying what we think gives us a wider conversational range than saying what we know." – Cullen Hightower, American humorist

Conversing Leaders

Leaders tend to believe that as they move up the hierarchy of an organization, they earn the right to speak exclusively to the masses. To some extent this is true, but most leaders tend to depend too much on mass communication. Such leaders operate under a flawed paradigm: (1) a leader addresses the organization at large, and, (2) those in the organization do what they are told. As anyone who has been "led" by one of these leaders knows, people do not fall in line that easily.

When leaders communicate by proclamation and edict they become disconnected from the individuals they lead and are less likely to lead them in meaningful ways. Employees view these leaders much as they would a newscaster – someone who merely reads words from a prepared statement. We don't believe the newscaster to be an expert in the area they speak of, or even passionate about what they proclaim. We simply see them as someone who is "doing their job" as a disinterested party. We don't connect with them. Leaders fall prey to the same perception if they fail to include sincere conversation in their leadership approach. They are seen as "doing their job" rather than establishing a genuine connection with their employees.

"Most conversations are simply monologues delivered in the presence of witnesses." – Margaret Millar, author

Strategic Conversations

The culture of an organization is expressed and reinforced through thousands of individual conversations. When leaders become disconnected from their team, the organizational culture suffers. A leader that attempts to lead by proclamation will create a shallow culture not able to withstand the pressures of growth or competition. Leaders and employees must interact with each other to create a purpose-centered culture. Conversations of today will build the culture of tomorrow. Culture and conversation depend on each other.

We are shaped by our daily conversations, which in turn shape the conversations we will have in the future. Conversations convey the history of an organization and describe the heroes of its past. Meaningful conversation creates a connection between those involved in the discussion. Through such dialogue we deepen friendships and learn to trust each other in more significant ways. This interaction of people and words is critical to an organization's development. Conversations are already taking place; leaders need only look for opportunities to participate in them. Leaders must be willing to invest time in conversation if they desire to influence others. The power to move an organization to new levels of success is dependent upon instructive, clarifying and encouraging conversations.

"The character of a man is known from his conversations."
Menander, Greek dramatist

The Four Conversations: Aligning People and Purpose

Successful leaders use conversation to align people with the purpose of their organization. These aligning conversations can be characterized by the four categories in the following exhibit. Placing individuals in one of four broad categories enables the leader to strategically guide them to a more engaged and supportive position.

As demonstrated in the following graphic, the leader places the individual on a matrix that measures his or her level of engagement on one axis, and their level of support on the other axis.

Four Conversations

Highly Supportive	Highly Supportive & Engaged ⭐
Not Supportive or Engaged	Highly Engaged

SUPPORTIVE ↑

ENGAGED ⟶

The best aligned organization is one that has the majority of its team members in the upper right, or *Highly Supportive & Engaged* box. A *Highly Supportive* individual is one who understands where the organization is headed and supports that effort with their words and attitudes. A *Highly Engaged* individual is an active force (but not a supportive one) within the organization. He or she lobbies for a particular position and is generally effective in bringing others to their point-of-view, although it may not align with the organization. As the matrix demonstrates, based on levels of engagement and support, an individual is placed in the corresponding box. The goal is a team that knows the purpose of the organization and supports it by their attitudes and actions.

This "placement" is subjective in many ways, but it serves as a point of departure for the leader to begin one-on-one conversations. The eventual goal is to bring those who are not highly supportive and highly engaged into that upper right hand box, and to retain those currently at that optimal level of engagement and support.

Each of the four categories or boxes corresponds to

distinctive personality characteristics. These are listed later to assist leaders in placement on the matrix. An example of each of the four conversations between an employee and his or her supervisor is found in the appendix. Several blank copies of the matrix are included in the final pages for you to plot your team.

66

"To listen closely and reply well is the highest perfection we are able to attain in the art of conversation." – Francois de La Rochefoucauld, French nobleman

Highly Supportive Characteristics

Those employees in the *Highly Supportive* category are generally supportive of the organizational purpose and leadership, but without extraordinarily productive activity. They are often consumed and distracted by the details of their work and rarely venture into new roles or develop new skills. They enjoy the status quo. A good day at work is one in which they "keep their head down" and focus on the task at hand. In short, they are not engaged.

When asked, they appreciate the opportunity to be part of the organization but rarely aspire to new positions or a higher level of performance. They have an underlying fear of losing their job and will be quick to say whatever they believe the leader wants to hear. For that reason, they are often seen as disingenuous by their co-workers.

With half of the desired characteristics in place (supportive but not engaged) this employee still presents a significant challenge. It is more difficult to move a supportive employee to the upper right box than an engaged employee. Engagement requires a high level of energy and mastery of interpersonal skills. Supportive employees often lack the ability to produce strategically focused energy and are fearful of developing interpersonal skills. Compared to *Highly Engaged* employees, *Highly Supportive* employees worry that a personal position or opinion may jeopardize their job.

66

"Conversation is an art in which a man has all mankind for his competitors, for it is that which all are practicing every day while they live." – Ralph Waldo Emerson, American author, poet and philosopher

Highly Engaged Characteristics

The *Highly Engaged* (but not supportive) individual has mastered the ability to pursue a cause and is an effective opinion leader among peers. He or she displays a defiant attitude toward leadership and is quick to challenge in public forums. Highly engaged persons don't necessarily disagree with the leader, but will oppose them to recruit other employees to their side. They seek respect and are able to enlist followers. They know the leverage points of the organization and use them strategically. However, despite their lack of support, they are a very valuable team member if they can become highly supportive.

If the *Highly Engaged* cannot be "brought onboard" they will be a disruptive force and must exit the organization. Through respectful conversations in which you listen intently to their ideas and give them a voice, they will often move to the *Highly Supportive & Engaged* box. These conversations should explore ways they can put their "fingerprint" on the organizational purpose. By doing so they save face with their supporters and create the appearance of a victory on behalf of the dissenters. Once engaged and supportive, they can take on leadership responsibilities if they have not ostracized the other *Highly Supportive & Engaged* employees.

❝

"Conversation is food for the soul." – Mexican Proverb

Not Supportive or Engaged Characteristics

Unfortunately, leaders spend a great deal of their effort and time on the *Not Supportive or Engaged* employees to the detriment of the *Highly Supportive & Engaged* team members. *Not Supportive or Engaged* individuals are "renters" as opposed to "owners." They often see their job as a means to a pay check. Quality and service are not important to them as these values require too much personal effort. They describe themselves as a loner or perhaps a member of a small group of like-minded "renters" who is passing through on the way to the next in a string of jobs. These individuals pose the greatest risk to an organization's legal compliance, quality performance and customer satisfaction. Other employees silently question why leaders allow them to stay in the organization. *Highly Supportive & Engaged* team members are personally offended by these employees and if forced to work closely with them, will often leave the organization. Characterized by low productivity, high lost work time, high levels of re-work, and low job satisfaction – these employees are difficult, yet not impossible, to bring to the upper right box.

It is critical to see the *Not Supportive or Engaged* employee as very resilient. They understand that human nature makes it difficult for many leaders to address unproductive, marginal employees. They are knowledgeable of human resource policies and procedures and quick to use them in their defense. They have endured patiently until a promotion moved previous supervisors out. Underneath their persona of apathy, however, like most people, they (1) want to be cared for and (2) they want to make a difference. It is likely the circumstances of their life or previous work experience has taught them to emotionally disconnect from people. By reaching out to them in these two areas (make them feel cared for and giving them an opportunity to make a difference), alignment with the company purpose is possible but difficult.

A caution however; since they must develop on two fronts – support and engagement – it is best to move them toward *Highly Supportive* and later work on their level of engagement. We will cover more about the timing of improvements later.

"

"Each person's life is lived as a series of conversations."
– Deborah Tannen, author and professor of linguistics

Highly Supportive & Engaged Characteristics

Highly Supportive & Engaged employees "get" the purpose of the organization. They are the role model to which you want others to aspire. They serve as a sounding board for your ideas and are confident enough to offer suggestions. They see the benefits of change. They understand the formal and informal processes of the enterprise. They create and use strong alliances and networks. Their peers recognize them as leaders and seek their support. They are a source of honest feedback concerning the direction of the organization as well as the state of employee morale.

The *Highly Supportive & Engaged*, however, are not without their detractors. As "rising stars" in the organization they will often be disliked by the *Highly Engaged* and the *Not Supportive or Engaged* individuals. Their level of support and engagement puts them at odds with the two bottom categories of the matrix. They are seen as "yes men" or women who use connectional power ("the boss said") to advance their position. As new leaders, their inability to develop consensus in the organization will hamper their overall effectiveness, but with time, they will learn to "endear" others to their leadership.

Characteristics

Highly Supportive	Highly Supportive & Engaged
• Agreement without action • Distracted by details • Seen as disingenuous • Fear of job loss	• Embrace the vision • Excellent role model • Disliked by Highly Engaged • Source of feedback
Not Supportive or Engaged	Highly Engaged
• "Renter" not "owner" • Risk to quality and service • Often a loner • Resilient	• Opinion Leader • Opposes management • Seeks respect • Interpersonal skills

SUPPORTIVE

ENGAGED

66

*"The real art of conversation is not only to
say the right thing at the right place but to leave unsaid
the wrong thing at the tempting moment."*
– Lady Dorothy Nevill,
British author, hostess and horticulturist

Talking Points

If each of the four employee (or volunteer, church member, partner) categories has differing points of view and needs, then it follows that each of the conversations with them will be a bit different. It is not easy to move employees between the categories, so a leader must be realistic. Not every individual will successfully relocate to the upper right box of the matrix. However, to fulfill the purpose of your organization you should not stop short of that goal.

Being engaged and supportive is a personal choice that each individual must make. It is important that you keep this principle of choice in mind and respect their decision. However, there is only one option for the employee to remain with the organization: they must be supportive <u>and</u>

engaged. Do not create the impression that other options exist. You should be careful and patient to explain why engaged and supportive is their only option. Speak about the purpose of the organization and the importance of their involvement in that effort. Express in a caring way your desire to include them and to help them make a difference in the organization. Seek out their personal strengths and strive to shape their role around those strengths. Reinforce that a bad "fit" in your organization does not mean they are a "bad" fit everywhere.

Remember that even though the prospect of moving an individual to another level will often seem daunting, it is possible. You should remain engaged and intent on discovering the best solution for the employee. By understanding their perspective, you turn a potentially difficult conversation into a beneficial change.

99

*"A single conversation with a wise man
is better than ten years of study." – Spanish Proverb*

Conversation 1: *Highly Supportive & Engaged*

There is a strategic sequence to the conversations beginning with *Highly Supportive & Engaged* employees. Once these conversations begin, there will be a high level of awareness among the employees that something is going on. This heightened awareness can be used to your advantage to focus the organization on change. By speaking with the role model employees first, you avoid leading them to believe a negative conversation is in store for them. As these conversations become routine, the sequence will become less important.

With *Highly Supportive & Engaged* individuals you should "re-recruit" them continually. They are the prized resources and highly desired by other organizations. Remind them of their value to the team and the bright future they have with your organization. Seek ways to better utilize their strengths. Look for the key intersecting points of both where they feel cared for and where they are making a difference. Ask how they would like to increase their strategic imprint on the organization. Understand what gives and takes energy from them as they perform their job. Offer them additional leadership training. Revisit times in the past that you have recognized them among their peers. Determine how they prefer to be recognized. Get their feedback on how you can better communicate with them. Have them describe frustrations and barriers they encounter in their work.

The conversation with the *Highly Supportive & Engaged* is an enjoyable exchange; however, listen very carefully for anything that might cause them to leave your organization. You depend on *Highly Supportive & Engaged* individuals. Do not take them for granted.

Conversation 2: *Highly Engaged*

Move next, on the first round, to the *Highly Engaged* employees. Be aware that they have spoken with their *Highly Supportive and Engaged* colleagues and fully expect to be "re-recruited" as well.

Begin by seeking their input on how they perceive their role in the organization. They will often acknowledge that they don't "see eye-to-eye" with you on all things. Encourage them to describe their role as it relates to the purpose of the organization. Ask them to explain how they align with the purpose of the company. Answer their questions respectfully and fully. Take care to show respect for their point of view. Ask them to give examples of their strengths and how they can be better used in the organization.

Describe the purpose of the organization and the value they provide if they choose to be supportive. Point out specific ways they can be more supportive. Ask if they are willing to support your leadership and the organization's purpose. To give them time to think about your request, schedule another meeting in 24 hours to hear their decision.

Conclude by expressing your desire for them to be a highly supportive member of the team.

In all categories, other than the *Highly Supportive & Engaged* employees, if they indicate in the follow-up meeting they are not willing to be supportive and/or engaged, let them know you respect their choice but you will follow your organization's progressive discipline policy since their current performance is not acceptable. Consult your Human Resource professional to set clear expectations and document their lack of performance. The employee will often seek other employment opportunities as they, perhaps for the first time, now understand what is expected of them and the conviction you have toward ensuring they are highly supportive and engaged.

Conversation 3: *Highly Supportive*

Highly Supportive employees will be very apprehensive about your meeting. Their tendency is to expect the worst: the loss of their job. Immediately calm their fears by expressing positive attributes about them or their performance. Expect them to be reluctant to be transparent for fear of reprisal. Eventually you can coax them to engage in a more open dialogue, but don't make them uncomfortable.

After calming their fears, describe the purpose of the organization as a "cause" that will energize them. Ask if that description sounds like something in which they can invest themselves. (Keep in mind they will generally agree with whatever you say – but getting them to talk is the key here.) Define their new role as being more energetic and engaged. Give them examples of how they can be more effective. Provide them with the same 24-hour follow-up to gauge their intentions but realize they will likely agree to anything. Use the follow-up meeting as encouragement to be more engaged over time. This conversation will be delicate as you paint them a picture of a highly engaged team member without aggressively challenging their present lack of engagement.

If they decide after the 24-hour period that they are not interested in doing what it takes to be engaged, remind them it is their only option if they wish to remain a member of the team and ask them to let you help rethink their career direction. Give them time as they will often decide that the prospect of finding another job is less desirable than striving to be more engaged. Encouragement is critical with this employee. It will take a tremendous change in their energy level. They will be fearful of the change. If they are willing to try, provide them the time and support they need.

Conversation 4: *Not Supportive or Engaged*

This brings you to the most carefully structured conversation of the four. Keep in mind the *Not Supportive or Engaged* employee is very resistant to management's pressure to change and is a veteran of "encouragement" to do a better job. To be effective in this conversation, stick strictly to setting a firm and clear expectation. Be clear they have only one option in your organization – to be highly supportive and engaged.

Be very careful to not praise them for any aspect of their performance. It is their nature to hear the praise and dismiss the criticism. Invite them to engage in the conversation and let them know why it is important they do so. Ask them to describe their goals compared to those of the organization. Listen carefully to where they would like to make a difference. Ask them to describe their strengths. This will be difficult for them. Don't get discouraged if they ignore the request.

Not Supportive or Engaged employees have grown accustom to remaining detached and unemotional to avoid accepting criticism or being accountable for their actions.

Expect them to direct attention to others or accuse you of singling them out. Ignore their attempt and focus only on your specific expectations of them. Explain that the goals they have described for themselves do not fit with the needs of the organization. Carefully describe the role, attitude and behavior that you will expect from them. Offer them the opportunity to ask clarifying questions. If their questions or comments are not about the expectations, lead them back to the point of discussion. Do not let them set the agenda or place you on the defensive.

Let them know the choice to become supportive and engaged is theirs to make, and if they desire to meet your expectation there is a place for them in the organization. Give them 24 hours to consider what is expected of them and to commit to your expectation. Be clear regarding your resolve. State if they do not desire to meet your expectations there will not be a role for them in the organization.

In the follow-up meeting they will likely stand firm using their detached approach and not offer you much hope for change. Work with your Human Resource professional to begin, or continue the process of progressive discipline.

Stay focused on the negative impact this type of employee brings to your organization as your motivation.

If they return with a sincere desire to become more engaged and supportive, begin first to increase their level of support. Give them time to master the supportive phase prior to moving on to becoming more engaged.

Talking Points

Highly Supportive	Highly Supportive & Engaged
• Calm their fear • Find their passion • Define their role • Give them a cause	• Re-recruit them • Enlarge their "imprint" • Recall times of recognition • Offer additional training
Not Supportive or Engaged	Highly Engaged
• Do not praise • Set clear expectations • Describe their only option • Ask them to be supportive	• Respect their view • Seek their support • Describe potential value • Listen carefully

SUPPORTIVE

ENGAGED →

Key Concepts:

- Aligned people fulfill purpose.
- Alignment by proclamation and decree is not effective in the long-run.
- Technology cannot replace verbal communication.
- The need for a leader to engage in one-on-one conversations does not diminish as they attain higher positions of leadership.
- We are shaped by our conversations which in turn shape our perspective and future conversations.
- Create links and associations between people through conversation.
- We are more likely to change our view and be supportive through one-on-one conversation.
- Conversations already exist. Leaders need only to look for opportunities to participate.
- Meaning and purpose should be core topics of the conversations.
- Transparency in conversation is critical to creating trust.
- Vocabulary is very important and context connects people with their role in the organization's purpose.

- Understanding another's perspective makes difficult conversations more effective.
- Look for ways to demonstrate that you care for the employee and help them make a difference in the organization.
- Make sure an employee understands the need to be highly supportive and engaged. Include specifics on why that is their only option.
- Some people have a tendency to ignore criticism in the presence of even a hint of encouragement.
- Remember that everyone makes a personal choice whether to fit or not fit with an organization's purpose.

"

*"Winning is important to me, but what brings me real joy
is the experience of being fully engaged in whatever I'm doing."*
– Phil Jackson, NBA coach, Los Angeles Lakers

Investing Time

The question of priorities and a leader's busy schedule
generally becomes an issue. Busy leaders see one-
on-one conversations as inconvenient to schedule and
burdensome to manage. They desire a wholesale approach
instead – "Line the employees up and let me proclaim my
expectations." The work of change can be challenging,
but the rewards are great. Don't give up.

You don't have to make more time for these conversations;
you merely have to re-allocate the time you have. Review
your time allocation in a given week or month; you'll
likely find you are spending much of your time on issues
caused by unsupportive and unengaged employees. Once
employees are aligned, your time is available for more
strategic pursuits and conversations. Often, up to 80% of
a leader's time is spent on issues or employees caused by

the misalignment of employee and purpose.

To produce change in the shortest time possible, an employee should be given 30-days to move from their present "box" to the next desired box.

30 Days to Change

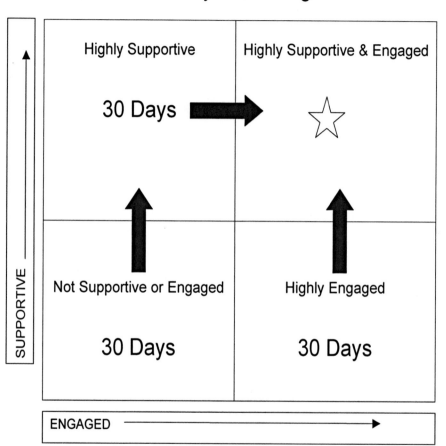

As noted earlier, the one exception to this 30-day goal is the *Not Supportive or Engaged* employee. They should be allowed 30 days to move to the *Highly Supportive* box and then additional 30 days to migrate to the *Highly Supportive & Engaged* box in a two-step approach. The *Highly Supportive* and the *Highly Engaged* employees should each be allowed 30 days to make their way into a *Highly Supportive & Engaged* position.

Thirty-days are given to reach the next desired box. This does not mean an employee has 30 days to decide whether or not they are committed to change. That decision should generally be reached within 24 hours of your initial, expectation-setting conversation. Once he or she commits to change, the 30-day period is aggressive enough to keep them moving, yet spacious enough to allow time to learn and demonstrate new behaviors. When communicating your expectations, be very clear and firm about your 30-day plan.

Next we come to the matter of how much of your time to invest in each of the four categories. The principle of financial investment should be your guide. Typically you would not invest in a stock if you did not anticipate a return on your investment. Comparably, invest in employees you anticipate will succeed. This is not to say you ignore someone that will take more work to reach the final goal. Most of your time should be invested in re-recruiting and supporting your *Highly Supportive & Engaged* employees. In fact, 75% of your time should be spent on the *Highly Supportive & Engaged*, and only 10% each invested in the *Highly Engaged* and *Highly Supportive* categories. Only 5% of your time should be invested in the *Not Supportive or Engaged* category.

While this allocation may seem harsh or indifferent to three of the four categories, take comfort in knowing that most employees recognize what it means to be supportive and engaged. They know what it will take to become more supportive or engaged without much involvement on your part. The difference now is in your conviction that they must change or exit the organization.

Investing Your Time

Highly Supportive 10%	Highly Supportive & Engaged 75%
Not Supportive or Engaged 5%	Highly Engaged 10%

SUPPORTIVE

ENGAGED →

As the low performing employees choose to move toward your expectation they should benefit from more of your leadership attention. Your investment in them should continue to increase as they move toward your expectation.

This brings us to the "what if". What if they don't move out of the organization on their own and refuse to be engaged and/or supportive? The answer is straight forward: for the overall sake of organizational purpose they must be removed from the organization. It is difficult for a leader to be a staunch defender of the organizational purpose and knowingly allow someone to undermine that purpose. Leaders must protect both the purpose and those who have chosen to pursue it.

If an employee is not willing to meet your expectation, you should engage your Human Resource professional to address the situation using your progressive discipline process. (If you are using the *Four Conversations* approach with volunteers in a non-profit organization, the progressive discipline process will not always apply. However, before removing the volunteer or member you should alert leaders of your Board of Directors or other oversight body of your intentions.)

It is commonplace for leaders in large corporations, small churches and volunteer agencies to tolerate a "disconnect" between the people within the organization and the purpose of the organization. These leaders believe an acceptable percentage of employees will remain unproductive, unsupportive and unengaged. This belief is an increasingly expensive and counter-productive obstacle that prevents the organization from effectively fulfilling its purpose.

Span of control also contributes to the success of the model. In my experience, I find it difficult for a leader to be effective if their direct report count exceeds twenty-five employees. The model requires a leader to engage in weekly conversations with their team. Even if for only ten minutes each week, these conversations keep the team members engaged and pointed toward the organizational purpose. It is virtually impossible for a leader to have meaningful conversations with more than twenty-five team members.

The twenty-five or less direct report rule challenges leaders to get creative in their organizational design to utilize team leaders or other supervisory positions. It is through these supervisors that employees will put a "face" on the organization. It is important that all employees interact with some level of supervisor regularly. Equally important is the skill with which these supervisors apply the principles of *Four Conversations* as well as other basic leadership principles. In other words, the title of "supervisor" does not make someone a leader. On-going training for you and your leadership team is critical.

Be a Self-Aware Leader

The success of the *Four Conversations* approach will depend on you, the leader. Some leaders are able to navigate the conversations with ease while others may struggle. Success depends largely on the individual leader's perspective and personality.

Many psychologists believe our personality changes very little beyond our infant years. We routinely react and interact in a set pattern after those formative years. Our approach toward people becomes predictable and natural. Yet, by being self-aware, we are able to manage our style to optimize our relationship with our team members.

In my experience, the greatest predictor of success with the *Four Conversations* approach is whether or not the leader has a high degree of self-awareness. A self-aware leader is one who is able to accurately perceive and predict how his or her words and actions will be interpreted by others. In other words, they have an innate ability to play out the story-line in advance.

I'm often amused, and annoyed, when I encounter people

who are not self-aware. They barge into the middle of a meeting loudly moving their chair or walking around the room visibly interrupting. Others talk loudly on their cell phone in the middle of a meeting. These unaware (or in some cases aware but uncaring) individuals signal that they are indifferent to the comfort, focus or feelings of others. In short, they are inconsiderate and disrespectful.

Self-aware leaders are different. As they interact with people, they immediately sense how their message is being received and they make real-time, almost imperceptible, adjustments in their vocabulary, body language and messaging. The self-aware leader is highly sensitive to the eco-system we call "organization" as well as the part they play in the unfolding journey toward organizational purpose. These leaders effectively navigate the sea of human emotions, expectations and connections.

A self-aware leader deeply understands the universal desire of all people for a caring environment that affords them the opportunity to make a difference. They understand the strength of building trust among those they lead. These special leaders see individual conversations as their most valuable leadership tool. By being careful not to expect preferential treatment, self-aware leaders avoid a prideful sense of being better than others.

There are many forces preventing a leader from becoming an effective, self-aware person. These forces stem from the tendency of leaders to be consumed by prideful behavior. This pride is not based upon an individual or group accomplishment; rather it is the pride that tempts every person to think of themselves as better than others. It is the opposite of humility. It is the enemy of a successful organization.

Humility is a virtue often misunderstood in our American culture of bravado and accomplishment. We perceive humility incorrectly as a sign of weakness; a sense that we must give in to the demands of others at the expense of our own desires. These definitions are incorrect. It has been accurately said that humility does not mean that we think less of ourselves; it simply means we think of ourselves less. A self-aware leader thinks less about what he desires and more about the desires of others. It is in that focus on others that genuine leaders thrive and pursue purpose.

American business practices and corporate folklore have

deepened this notion of special prominence for leaders. We are led to believe that an organization is highly dependent upon the "rock star" leader who is deemed worthy of status and fame. Set apart from the organization as beacons of intelligence and inspiration, these "leaders" are lauded on the cover of business magazines. However, in the opinion of the organization's employees, that self-consumed leader is far from inspirational. In fact, such a prideful placeholder of a leadership position is not a leader at all. Leaders attract others who naturally desire to follow them in pursuit of something important.

Pride convinces a leader that he or she deserves the trappings of power afforded by position. Special privileges, reserved parking, executive dining rooms, personal drivers – all of these communicate to the organization that the leader is set above the team. These differentiating perks make if difficult, if not impossible, for a leader to genuinely connect with team members in any meaningful way.

As a self-aware leader it is your responsibility to enter each individual conversation with a sense that everyone on the team is valuable and has something to add to the organization's success. You must be (not merely act) genuine, compassionate and trusted. By seeking ways to communicate your care for others and by searching out ways for every person to make a difference, you naturally become a self-aware leader. Individuals in your organization naturally follow. In the end, you "endear" others to your leadership.

Endearing Leaders

There is a difference between a boss and a leader – a big difference. Unfortunately, the business press coverage of high flying Wall Street executives mischaracterizes leadership.

To effectively employ the *Four Conversation* approach, a leader must genuinely be interested in placing his or her team in a role that plays to their strengths and allows them the freedom to pursue the organization's purpose. This special leader must strive to "endear" the team to his or her leadership. Self-absorbed leaders will not succeed at using the *Four Conversations*.

A leader that endears others to his or her leadership is highly self-aware of the impact of their vocabulary, actions and intentions. They are careful not to create an air of arrogance with the trappings of power normally associated with senior leaders. Transparency in their intentions will endear their team to their trustworthy encouragement and genuine concern.

The conversational leader must pursue the craft of engaging

others in productive and uplifting dialogue. Listening to others must be a highly developed skill of the endearing leader. A sensitivity to others that conveys you are more interested in what they have to say than what you would like to say is critical. Many practices and symbols exist in the organization that will falsely reinforce a leader's value as greater than that of the employee. The endearing leader must continually be on guard against diminishing the importance of others on the team.

Popular business books offer many short-cuts to effective leadership. Some offer simple steps that focus more on business processes and strategy than on the people involved. Financial measures and productivity improvements, while important, have all too often relegated people to little more than an interchangeable cog in the wheel – easily replaced when necessary. Process cannot replace people. As endearing leaders, we must return to an era of valuing the individual, placing them in a role that complements their strengths and affords them creative latitude in the journey toward the desired outcome.

The *Four Conversations* approach will enable willing leaders to reconnect with individuals in a manner that respects talent, encourages aspirations and unifies the organization around purpose. However, the approach also requires something from the employee – they must possess the ability and desire to be highly engaged and supportive. The process starts with the crucial focus on hiring the right person for the job.

Hiring for Engagement and Support

To a certain extent, an "engaged" person has always been so. They were likely engaged in school; participating in extracurricular activities and sports. Comfortable with serving in leadership roles, they seemed to naturally fall into the right positions.

This is not to say that engagement cannot be taught or improved. However, it is far more efficient to hire for engagement than try to change someone's core personality. Personality cannot change in drastic measures. Therefore employee selection is critical to quickly build a highly engaged and supportive team.

Passion drives engagement. People naturally engage in whatever fuels their passion. A passionate person will be naturally supportive as well. That is the beauty of passion. As you hire people with a passion for your purpose, you will automatically select people who are engaged in and supportive of your purpose.

Look at prospective employees through the lens of passion. Have they demonstrated a passion for a social or religious cause? Do they volunteer at a non-profit? Have they served the under-privileged? Have they overcome a traumatic event or achieved a great accomplishment? In short, look for signs of passion as an indicator of a capacity to be passionate. Some people have chosen to ignore their calling in life. They will likely ignore the purpose of your organization as well.

When you find a person of talent, passion and creativity – hang on to that person! The act of "re-recruiting" introduced earlier means just that; a continual recruitment effort to ensure they do not leave. Continue to "sell" them on the merits of your organization. Ask them about their desired future and help them achieve it. Talk to them about what is working and what you can do differently to make their role more meaningful. Understand how they like to be recognized. Get their input on your strategy. Listen to them as they discuss customer feedback. Spend time with them. Acknowledge their progress. Ask them for their continued support. They value time spent with you, the leader. You should equally value time with them.

Engagement and support, when properly linked, are essential to organizational success. Unfortunately, many organizations have grown to believe that some disconnect in engagement, support or both is to be expected. Each passing year, these organizations accept as routine, a higher and higher percentage of disconnected employees. Service suffers. Turn-over is high. Good employees leave out of frustration. Profits plunge while senior leaders search for salvation in the next strategy or process improvement. Engagement and support should be a key focus of the leader.

The principles of *Four Conversations* enable you to return to the basics of engagement and support. They are irreplaceable as the underlying foundation for success.

An Engaged and Supportive Future

The *Four Conversations* properly used will positively change your organization as individual conversations become the fabric of your leadership style and the engine of organizational purpose. Your vocabulary of expectation, accountability and purpose becomes the dialect of the organization. Your team understands and readily expresses to others what it means to engage and support the enterprise purpose. Dialogue is supported with genuine emotions and personal choices are expected. Actions are aligned and not wasted. An intense desire to improve is shared among team members.

As a leader, you move from your dependence on technology (emails, text messaging, videos, etc.) to one-on-one conversations that convey your message. You grow comfortable with this kind of personal interaction and learn something from each exchange. A self-aware approach is brought to all of your conversations. You use emotional stories; you are transparent to your team and trusted to do as you have promised. Issues are uncovered far sooner than they might be as your conversations reveal early signs of misalignment. You teach others to be comfortable in their ability to lead through conversation, and the organization benefits greatly from that skill. You are acutely aware of the connection between emotion, vocabulary and context.

Conversation has indeed become a lost art in the race to be bigger, faster and more profitable. As a result, leaders no longer hear the faint voice of their team. The conversational leader can change that emphasis and make a difference in the lives of those who naturally follow their leadership. A caring culture based on dialogue will reconnect people and purpose. The conversation awaits you. Lead.

66

"I often quote myself. It adds spice to my conversation." – George Bernard Shaw, playwright and author

Appendix

Example Conversations

Each of the four conversations requires a slightly different approach. Each of the following examples is given to help you envision the content and flow. Your natural style will, of course, impact your personal approach; however, it is recommended that you stay within the framework of the examples in order to have the most impact.

Conversation #1: *Highly Supportive & Engaged* – Jim and Cara

As Jim made his way down the hall to the office of his boss, he wondered what would prompt Cara to schedule a formal meeting. Cara usually just stopped by to say "Hi" and ask how it was going. His thoughts raced back over the last couple of weeks to look for problems with his performance that might be the topic of the meeting. His last evaluation was pretty good and he thought he had a good relationship with Cara. His pace quickened as he neared her office.

Pausing at the boss's door, Jim took a deep breath, knocked and entered. "Good morning Cara are you ready for me?"

Looking up from her desk, Cara flashed a big smile. "Yes, good morning Jim, thank you for meeting with me. I know it's a little unusual for us to have a set meeting time but I wanted let you know how much I appreciate you. Please, sit down."

As Jim reached to take a chair in front of her desk, Cara quickly came around the desk to sit next to Jim. *Odd*, thought Jim, but he was relieved to hear it wasn't going to be bad news. He needed his job and didn't really want to leave the company.

"I know I don't tell you this nearly enough," began Cara, "but you are one of the top performers of our company and you should be very proud of what you have accomplished. I know I'm very proud of you Jim."

"Wow," Jim said with a bit of bewilderment in his voice, "I really appreciate that. I enjoy my job and I really like working for you. I do feel like I have something valuable to offer the company."

Cara agreed, "You do have a lot to offer Jim, and part of what I want to accomplish today is to make sure we are using your strengths so you can continue to be highly engaged and supportive of our purpose. Your team has led the company in satisfaction scores 8 of the last 12 months and I've got to tell you how much I enjoyed giving you that banner in front of your peers. You are doing a tremendous job and I want to make sure you are happy here. If you don't mind, I have a few questions for you to help me support you and be a resource to your success. Would that be OK?"

"Well, sure, I'm happy doing what I'm doing and I can't think of anything you can do differently, but fire away if you like," replied Jim.

Cara began, "Well for starters, I want to make sure I am properly applying your strengths to our company's purpose. What do you think your strengths are? What is it that gets you excited, gives you energy?"

Jim hesitated, grasping for an appropriate answer, "I really haven't thought of it that way but I really like interacting with our customers; especially the one's that have questions about our service. I feel good about walking them through the solutions we bring and getting that immediate sense of accomplishment as their questions are answered. I'll admit, on the days that I'm assigned to do paperwork, it zaps a lot of my energy. I just don't feel like I accomplish much. I know the forms and filing are important, but it's just not me. I do it, but I don't love it."

Cara nodded in approval. "You are very good at the customer relations side of our business. If that is the strength you want to focus on then let's talk about how we do that. In the end, I want you to wake up every morning feeling like I care about you and that you make a difference. Over the next couple of weeks, I'd like for you to help our team automate the paperwork that is needed and review areas of the documentation process we can discontinue or reduce. I'd like to cut the time you are currently spending on paperwork by 75%. Looking to the future, I'd like to rely on you, Jim, as the customer service trainer for the rest of our team. To prepare you for that challenge, I'd like to enroll you in this course that I came across that is a sort of train-the-trainer class. How's that sound to you?"

"That sounds incredible Cara. It sounds like something that utilizes my strengths and I would really appreciate the opportunity," Jim said as his voice crackled with emotion a bit.

"Good, consider it done," said Cara. "Jim, where else would you like to put your mark on the company? What area can we focus on to maximize your strategic imprint on what we are doing around here?"

"It may sound a little weird," began Jim, "but I've always had an interest in film making, and I think it would be interesting to put together a documentary film of sorts where I interview some of our key customers about their purpose and how we can better serve them in reaching it. I don't think the budget would be much and I already have the video camera and lights – silly idea though, now that I say it out loud."

"No, not at all," Cara said quickly, "I think it is an awesome idea. We lose sight of what our customers are trying to accomplish and how we support that effort. I can see using that documentary as a training tool for our team. You could also use it in your customer service training we just spoke of. Great idea. I'd like you to come to our next senior leader meeting to discuss the concept. Let's plan on getting started in the next couple of weeks."

"Seriously Cara," Jim responded," that would be so great if I could do that. I love this place and just want to make it a better company. I appreciate all you are doing for me."

"You are very welcome Jim; you deserve to get the best from us because you consistently give us your best. I personally, appreciate all you do and I count it a privilege to be on your team. I want to make sure that I support you and that I'm not a barrier or hindrance to what you are accomplishing. Is there anything I can do to better communicate with you, remove barriers or frustrations you have?"

"I can't think of anything," Jim said as he looked at the floor, "other than, well, you asked – some times the emails you send me asking a question seem, well, a little harsh. I know I'm probably reading too much into the shortness of the note, but it just seems a little cold. I know you are busy and the short email works for you, but I'll admit that I'm very sensitive to what you say, do and write. If you are upset with me, I hope you will let me know."

Cara cringed a little as she listened to Jim. She knew that emails can create an unintended tone. "Jim, I'm very sorry my emails gave you that impression. Let's agree on two things: First, I will give you more background in my emails and make them more personable, and finally, you have my promise that if there is ever anything that you have done that causes me concern, we will talk about it in person. Fair enough?"

"Very fair," Jim said smiling, "it was no big deal, just thought I'd bring it up."

Cara stood to shake Jim's hand, "If it's important to you Jim, then it is very important to me. You are one of our stars and I consider it my privilege to make sure you are happy and engaged. I appreciate all the support you have shown me and I look forward to getting these things in play that we discussed today. I'd also like to make these little chats part of our routine."

"That would be great," Jim said as he stood, "I will do

whatever it takes to make the company successful and I really appreciate the support you have shown me Cara."

"My pleasure," Cara replied. "Let me know how I can help you and have a great day!"

I already have, thought Jim as he made his way back up the hall.

Conversation #2: *Highly Engaged* – Andy and Cara

Andy had prepared for his meeting with Cara for days. She had been his boss for about six months now and he had expected this meeting. As he drove to work he thought through his approach with her. She would likely give him the old sandwich: a compliment followed by a smack upside the head with a "weakness" that he needed to address, ending with a meaningless throw-down compliment. He would be ready. After all, he had been through this routine before and Cara was a novice. Like the previous six managers before her, he would eventually wait her out as she went on to pursue other opportunities.

He dropped his stuff off at his desk and then headed right

to Cara's wing of the building. "I'm here to see Cara. She is expecting me." He confidently told her secretary. "She will see you now," came the reply.

"Andy, good to see you," Cara greeted as Andy cautiously eased into the room. "Please sit down. Can I get you coffee, water?"

"Uh, no thanks Cara," he said confused by Cara's display of kindness. "I'm good. So, what's with the meeting today?"

"You always like to get right to it, don't you Andy? Well, let's do. The reason I want to meet with you is that I'm meeting with some of my key people to get their assessment of where we are as a company. I'd like your input. How are things going with you and your role here?

Andy stared at her a moment trying to figure out her angle. "Well, I think things are going OK. As good as can be expected. I understand you're new to the job and we don't agree on everything, but I work through it.

Cara leaned in and replied, "Andy you play a significant

role here, but I think we can utilize your strengths even more. The odd thing about strengths is that only you know what they are for you; only you know what gives you energy. I'd like to make use of them, but I'm not exactly sure what they are and how they fit. Can you help me with that? Do you understand what I mean?

Andy grew impatient. "Cara I have no idea what you're talking about. I show up. I work hard. And now you tell me that I don't fit the company mold. I've done a lot for this company. People respect me. They listen to me. If I tell them Cara is an OK person, then they believe it. If I tell them Cara doesn't have a clue, then they will ignore you."

"Slow down Andy," Cara interrupted. "I didn't say you don't fit in. I said that you not only fit in, but I think you have strengths that can be even more beneficial to our company. You are a leader among your peers. They do listen to you. I think that is a wonderful quality that you have and I'd like to work with you to use that influence even more. The part that is missing is your support of the overall purpose of the company. At times, you seem to pursue your own purpose, even when it is at odds with the company. Let me give you an example. Two weeks ago we had an important meeting scheduled to develop our strategic plan for next year. I would have liked to have your input in the meeting because I think you have good ideas, but instead you sat at the back of the room cracking jokes with those around you. I need you on the team Andy. You could be a very influential leader, but if you are leading our team in a different direction, then we can't exist that way. Can I count on you to be more supportive in the future Andy?

"I do a good job," Andy mumbled back in Cara's direction.

Cara stopped him, "I'm not talking about being an employee who simply does a job Andy. I'm asking you to sign up to be a leader in this organization who supports our purpose of providing the best service possible to our clients. You have the ability to do it, Andy. I'd like very much for you to be on the team, but I won't force you. It is your decision and if you decide that it is not right for you, that is your choice and I will respect you and your decision. I'd like for us to meet this time tomorrow and between now and then I'd like you to give our conversation some serious thought.

My request is that you become a supportive leader of this organization. When we get back together in 24 hours, I'd like to hear your decision. I appreciate your time today and look forward to hearing from you tomorrow." Cara stood and walked toward the office door.

Andy eased from his chair and headed back to his desk. The meeting wasn't what he had expected at all. *Guess I have a big decision ahead of me,* He thought as he walked down the hall.

Conversation #3: *Highly Supportive* – Jill and Cara

Headache and nausea had plagued Jill's morning. Her boss, Cara, asked to meet with her and that couldn't be good. Jill thought about her bills that were due and how hard it would be to find another job if she got fired. She had heard this sort of "pink slip" event usually happens on Friday, and today was Friday after all. But, the time had come for the meeting. She headed to Cara's office like an inmate headed to an execution.

The door to Cara's office creaked a little as Jill nudged it open and faintly called out, "Cara, did you want to see me now?"

"Jill, come in," Cara cheerfully called out, "I appreciate you meeting with me."

"My pleasure boss, anything you want," was the soft reply from Jill. "I'll admit I'm a little nervous, if this means bad news, I'd rather you get right to it."

Cara smiled and chucked, "Jill, please relax. There isn't going to be any bad news today. I want you to assist me with a cause that is special to me and I think it will be special to you. I think we have the opportunity to make our team the best in the company. By taking a new approach that is focused on the customer and their needs, I think we can create some exciting results together."

Jill nodded that she understood.

Cara continued, "Jill you have always been very supportive of me and the company. I greatly appreciate that about you. I never have to doubt whose side you are on. I haven't told you that near enough. And if you choose to support me in this new cause, I think we will make a great team. To do so, though, Jill, will take a new approach from you. I believe in you and I'm confident you can do it with a little coaching from me. I need you to get even more engaged in the purpose of our company. That means you'll need to have more face-to-face time with our key customers and I'll need you to do some training with our new employees. I'll also need you to share with me those great ideas that you have. I know that some of those things might be uncomfortable for you at first, but I've seen you work miracles with some of our unsatisfied customers and the way you trained Kendra in her new role was very impressive. It will take a higher level of energy from you, Jill, and you will have to take some risks, but I believe in you. I really would like you to consider it. Take some time to think it over and let's get back together tomorrow to see if you have questions about what I'm asking you to do. Sound good?"

"Sure Cara," Jill replied with apprehension. "I'll think about it. Whatever you want is fine with me."

"Thank you," Cara said as she leaned toward Jill. "I believe in you. I want you to really give it some thought. Don't just agree with whatever I ask, but think about what taking on this challenge can mean for the new Jill and the prospects for our team. Really think about it Jill. Will you do that for me?

Jill nodded as she and Cara stood.

As Jill lay in bed that night she thought about what Cara had to say. She wondered if she could be someone different at work. She really would like to step up and be a leader in the company. If only she could believe in herself like Cara believed in her. If only she could be the kind of leader Cara described.

Conversation #4: *Not Supportive or Engaged* – Dayton and Cara

Dayton had been through this drill several times. It was that time of the year when the boss puts the screws to the little guy just trying to get by. There was probably a name for the process, Dayton thought, or maybe even a greeting card for the special occasion.

Sitting in a chair waiting for Cara to come back in the office with the "complementary" water, Dayton glanced around the room. Typical head honcho stuff like awards, a picture of Mr. Boss, some long-titled books on leadership, management, and how to kick the snot out of the little guy just trying to make a buck.

"Dayton," Cara began as she re-entered the room and sat behind her desk, "let's get right to the point. I'm trying to place you in the best possible place for your strengths and interests. I'd like for you to share with me what your goals are and how you believe they fit with our company purpose.

Dayton saw this as a land mine and tried to tip-toe around it. "Look Cara, my primary goal is to stay out of your way and take home a few bucks each week to pay the bills."

Cara set silently a moment to let Dayton's description of his "goals" resonate with him. "That's not a goal that will get us where we need to be as a team Dayton. It doesn't fit with where we need to go. I don't think you are serious about the purpose we are striving to fulfill here, or about developing your career."

"Hold on Cara," Dayton shot back, "Are you telling me

that you are coming down on me when you've got a bunch of people sitting around here that do less than I do? They don't show up on time but I'm here doing my thing. They are ripping you off every time you turn around. But you're making me the target of your little "witch hunt" today?

Cara calmly went on. "Dayton, this isn't about anyone else. It is about you. I need you to be supportive of our purpose and engaged in the pursuit of that purpose. At the moment you are neither supportive nor engaged. I believe you can get there, but it will take a lot of work. Only you can decide whether or not you will pursue this goal. Everyone wakes up each day and decides what purpose they will serve. Some options are right for you and others are not. We each make choices. I will respect your choice if you decide this company is not right for you, but you must decide. You have 24 hours to think it over. This time tomorrow we will get back together, at which time you'll need to tell me what you have decided. If you choose not to decide, then I will decide for you. Is that clear Dayton?

"Whatever." Dayton snapped with a growl and left the office.

Cara sat there a moment. She wasn't surprised by Dayton's reaction.

A Note of Thanks

Like you, I am a product of my conversations and relationships. Without these special people, my life would be empty and without a message. My story reflects bits of their story. There are many to which I am grateful for allowing me to test my ideas and develop the premise of this book.

To my friends, past and present, at Memorial Hermann, I appreciate the trust you have placed in me for so many years. Doug, Dan, Chuck, Carrol, and Dale – you will likely see your fingerprints on many of these pages. Carla, Jennifer and Pranika, thanks for providing structure and guidance related to the "road show" that emerged. Louis and Tom, I appreciate the thoughtful reading and constructive comments.

To my publishers, Casey and Steph, thank you for nurturing this project from words on paper to a final project.

Leigh, thank you for bringing life and order to the words.

Jason, I appreciate the thoughtful way you worked through

early versions and the continual supply of articles and insights you feed me.

To my parents, thanks for the many years of "OTJ" training in the various business pursuits of "Brace, Inc." It was more educational than my degrees.

Diana, your constant encouragement and companionship is the bedrock of all I write, do and say. Thank you for the now 28 years of "no regrets" living.

And finally, in the same manner as my first book, *Simplify*, I write this book for my sons Ryan and Jordan – and welcome to these pages my newest child – daughter-in-law Janna. You all will be leaders in whatever you pursue. Your heart for what is more important than position or wealth is evident – you believe in people and the conversations they deserve.

Thanks to all!
Rod Brace

Rod Brace is a healthcare executive
in Houston, Texas

Continue the conversation at:
www.rodbrace.com

Also available by Rod Brace
Simplify: Releasing the Grip of Popular Culture

Four Conversations

	Highly Supportive	Highly Supportive & Engaged
SUPPORTIVE ↑	Not Supportive or Engaged	Highly Engaged

ENGAGED →

Four Conversations

Highly Supportive	Highly Supportive & Engaged
Not Supportive or Engaged	Highly Engaged

SUPPORTIVE ↑

ENGAGED →

Four Conversations

Highly Supportive	Highly Supportive & Engaged
Not Supportive or Engaged	Highly Engaged

SUPPORTIVE →

ENGAGED →

Four Conversations

Highly Supportive	Highly Supportive & Engaged
Not Supportive or Engaged	Highly Engaged

SUPPORTIVE →

ENGAGED →

Four Conversations

	Highly Supportive	Highly Supportive & Engaged
SUPPORTIVE ↑	Not Supportive or Engaged	Highly Engaged

ENGAGED →

Four Conversations

Highly Supportive	Highly Supportive & Engaged
Not Supportive or Engaged	Highly Engaged

SUPPORTIVE →

ENGAGED →

CPSIA information can be obtained at www.ICGtesting.com
Printed in the USA
BVOW021946190613

323779BV00004B/9/P